七夕

**Customs, Traditions and Landmarks |
Non-Fiction Series**

Copyright © 2022 by Level Learning, INC. and Washington Yu Ying PCS™
Original and Edited Text Copyright © 2022 by Washington Yu Ying PCS™

All rights reserved. No part of this book in whole or part may be reproduced without written permission from the publisher.

Published by Level Learning, INC.

Content Contributors:
Washington Yu Ying PCS™
Level Learning - Ya-Ching Chang

Illustrations by: Josh Taira

Leveling classification based on Level Learning standard.
For full description, visit www.levellearning.com

ISBN 978-1-64040-022-1
Simplified Chinese Edition

About Level Learning:
Level Learning provides a literacy focused curriculum specifically designed for K-12 Chinese as a Second Language classrooms. Our program offers 20 levels of specific and detailed objectives, leveled texts and passages, mastery-based online assessment, and analytics to enable data-driven instruction. Level Learning reading curriculum for both literature and informational text emphasize grammar and comprehension skills to help teachers develop confident and independent Chinese language readers. The non-fiction series of books are specifically designed to support our informational text course based on multiple national standards. To learn more about our entire offering, visit www.levellearning.com.

About Washington Yu Ying PCS™:
Washington Yu Ying PCS is a Mandarin English dual language immersion International Baccalaureate (IB) World school. Yu Ying's mission is to inspire and prepare young people to create a better world by challenging them to reach their full potential in a nurturing Chinese/English educational environment. Yu Ying's comprehensive IB, dual immersion curriculum equips students with global competencies for success in the real world. As a leader in immersion education, Yu Ying is determined to advance Chinese language programs and global citizenry education by helping other schools create and strengthen their Chinese programs. For more information, email: products@washingtonyuying.org

每年农历七月初七是中国的情人节，这一天也被称为"七夕"。七夕是中国的一个传统节日，也是一个很浪漫的节日。每年的七夕，大家都会想起牛郎和织女的传说。

传说，天上有一位叫织女的仙女。织女不但长得很漂亮，还会织布。她织的布就像天上的云彩一样美。但是，时间长了，织女觉得每天织布的日子很无聊。

有一天,织女偷偷来到人间游玩,遇到了一个叫牛郎的年轻人,他们很快相爱了。织女决定留在人间,和牛郎在一起。他们结婚后生活得很幸福,还生了两个孩子。

可是,织女的母亲知道后非常生气,她认为神仙和人是不能结婚的。织女因此被母亲带回天上,牛郎也为了织女而追到天上。织女的母亲看到牛郎来了,就在天上画了一条天河,让牛郎和织女站在天河的两边。他们只能看着天河的另一边,却不能见面。

天上的喜鹊知道了这件事，它们被牛郎和织女的爱情故事感动了，想要帮助牛郎和织女见面。成千上万的喜鹊飞来，在天河上搭成一座鹊桥，让牛郎织女能够见面。织女的母亲看到了，只好同意每年的七月初七，让牛郎和织女在鹊桥上见面。

因为牛郎和织女的爱情传说,在七夕这一天,很多女孩子都会动手做针线手工,希望自己能像织女一样有一双巧手。很多爱人之间也会互相送礼物,表达爱意。

在七夕的晚上，女孩子们会在院子里摆上瓜果点心，对着天上的牛郎星和织女星许愿，希望自己能像他们一样，有美好的爱情。

人们说七夕的晚上一定会下雨，那场雨是牛郎和织女每年见一次面所流下的眼泪。在七夕的晚上，抬头看看天空，也许你会看见牛郎和织女站在喜鹊搭成的桥上呢！

Glossary

	Pinyin	English Definition
农历	nóng lì	lunar calendar
情人节	qíng rén jié	Valentine's Day
传统	chuán tǒng	tradition
浪漫	làng màn	romantic
牛郎	niú láng	cowherd
织女	zhī nǚ	weaver girl
传说	chuán shuō	legend, myth
仙女	xiān nǚ	fairy
漂亮	piào liang	beautiful
织	zhī	to weave
布	bù	cloth
云彩	yún cai	cloud
无聊	wú liáo	bored
偷偷	tōu tōu	secretly
人间	rén jiān	the mortal world

	Pinyin	English Definition
游玩	yóu wán	to play
遇到	yù dào	to meet, encounter
年轻	nián qīng	young
相爱	xiāng ài	in love
决定	jué dìng	to decide
结婚	jié hūn	to marry
生活	shēng huó	to live
幸福	xìng fú	happy
母亲	mǔ qīn	mother
神仙	shén xiān	immortal god or goddess
天河	tiān hé	river in the sky
见面	jiàn miàn	to meet
喜鹊	xǐ què	Magpie, a type of bird
爱情	ài qíng	love
感动	gǎn dòng	to move emotionally

	Pinyin	English Definition
帮助	bāng zhù	to help
成千上万	chéng qiān shàng wàn	thousands and thousands
搭	dā	to build
桥	qiáo	bridge
同意	tóng yì	to agree
针线	zhēn xiàn	sewing needle and thread
手工	shǒu gōng	crafts
巧手	qiǎo shǒu	skillful
互相	hù xiāng	each other
摆	bǎi	to put
瓜果点心	guā guǒ diǎn xin	fruits and snacks
许愿	xǔ yuàn	to wish
眼泪	yǎn lèi	tears
抬头	tái tóu	look up

www.ingramcontent.com/pod-product-compliance
Lightning Source LLC
Chambersburg PA
CBHW041221070526
44584CB00001B/46